How to Trade
The ZUP indicator

Dana DeCecco

Dana is a former Commodity Trading Advisor

and 20 year independent trader

DEDICATION

Dedicated to the GOOD LORD

CONTENTS

ACKNOWLEDGMENTS

MT 4 Charting Platform
FreeStockCharts.com

Scott Carney and Larry Pesavento for
their work on harmonic patterns

1 THE ZUP INDICATOR

In 1935 H.M. Gartley published a book entitled "Profits in the Stock Market". Since then the pattern has been refined with additional parameters added, specifically Fibonacci retracement ratios. Gartley patterns are visible and measurable patterns that occur on technical analysis charts of various markets. These patterns apply to the Stock Market, the Commodities Market, and the Currency Market.

The Fibonacci based patterns can create bullish and bearish trading signals. The patterns must meet specific conditions to be considered a verified pattern. Key Fibonacci ratios are used to observe patterns that resemble and are similar to deformed "W" or "M" patterns within the chart. These patterns can be viewed on a few websites that can be found with a simple search. Other patterns have been developed that are similar to the Gartley pattern. They have been given names such as The Crab, The Bat, and The Butterfly.

The patterns consist of four distinct price points or pivot points on a price chart. They are considered classic retracement patterns and occur in all time frames. This makes these patterns usable for day traders, swing traders, and longer term investors. Gartley originally used ratios of one third and two thirds. It was not until further development of the pattern that the Fibonacci ratios were applied.

Gartley wrote that the pattern was successful approximately 70% of the time. Recent studies have reinforced this estimate. The pattern has been tested over the past 70 years making it a very reliable trading signal.

Larry Pesavento, a veteran trader of over 40 years, has done extensive research on this pattern. He published a book in 997 called "Fibonacci Patterns with Pattern Recognition".

When the pattern is properly identified, the trader can enter a high probability trade. The main advantage of this trade is the ability to set tight stop loss orders in case of pattern failure. As with any trading system, this pattern is best used in conjunction with other reinforcing indicators. Support, resistance, and pivot points would be an example of this.

This style of trading is sometimes referred to as Harmonic Trading. No trading systems work all of the time. A 70% win rate with a controlled risk makes this pattern based system an excellent trading system for many types of traders.

This is a universal trading indicator and can be applied to any market. Stocks, Forex and futures are examples of these markets. Since this indicator is published and available to the MT-4 Forex trading platform we will provide forex examples throughout this publication.

I also provide a professional trading system to give you a real edge in the marketplace. This technical trading system is used by banks, trading syndicates, hedge funds, and nearly every trader at a professional level.

Anyone with modest intelligence and a little discipline can trade this system. I will show you one step at a time how to use this forex trading system. The Simple Trading System works for forex spot trading and binary options trading.

I am not a software engineer. The signal software was developed by others. I am an experienced trader. When I discovered the incredible Fibonacci software, I developed the system to fit the software.

There are no secret "holy grail" trading methods. Think about it. The more traders that use a system, the better it works! Of course the Central Banks will set a currency price at will. We can't second guess the Central Banks but we do know when they trade and we can choose not to trade at that time. The Forex markets are open 24/5 so we can select our trading times.

No trading method is easy and I'm not saying this is easy. The problem with most novice traders is that they are lazy! That's why they get into this business...looking for easy money. There is no easy money but there are profits if you are willing to do the simple tasks that I will show you. Well....are you willing?

You can read all about Leonardo Fibonacci on the internet. The bottom line is that he developed a sequence of numbers found throughout nature. These ratios have been applied successfully to trading charts. Every charting program out there provides Fibonacci tools.

The markets tend to obey these ratios for reasons unknown. I don't much care about why it works. I do care about if it works. Traders must realize, if you find something that is working, then go with it. You do not need to analyze the WHY.

The "powers that be" are able and willing to manipulate the markets at will. They have very deep pockets and can bury us at will. If you can't beat them...join them.

Most of the trading in all markets is program trading. Computers are programmed to make the trades. What does a computer need? RULES !

The rules they follow are whatever they are instructed to follow. That is why your favorite indicator will work fine one day and not the next. Big money rules!

But there are certain rules that are universally followed (most of the time). These rules are SUPPORT, RESISTANCE, and FIBONACCI. Trend lines also get a piece of the act.

When you combine the effect of these universal indicators to price action you end up with a high probability trading system. Trading is all about probabilities. There is no such thing as a 100% accurate system.

Our Fibonacci indicator is called the ZUP , that stands for ZigZag universal with Pesavento patterns. If you want to read about this indicator go to: http://articles.mql4.com/376

ZUP - Universal ZigZag with Pesavento Patterns. Part 1[ru]

Introduction

Everybody who takes working on financial markets seriously, start creation of their individual trading systems earlier or later. The author of this present article created ZUP, ZigZag Universal with Pesavento Patterns as a result of this search. The MetaQuotes Software Corp. suggested me writing an article about this indicator. This present article is the first attempt to do it. In this and in the successive articles, I will describe the features of indicator ZUP, version 60 (ZUP_v60).

This indicator combines the Fibonacci sequence with the zig zag indicator. The results are uncanny. In 20 years of trading I have never seen a more accurate forecast. However, indicators will do you no good if you don't know how to trade them.

I will show you how to trade this indicator and develop a profitable trading system. The best way to convey this information is through charts and examples.

The MT-4 forex trading platform is available from most brokers. I suggest you use Oanda FX Trade because they provide reliable data. There is no minimum deposit with this broker.

Since MT-4 has upgraded their platform many of the ZUP algorithms are no longer functioning. I will provide a link for you to download the ZUP 113 which is functional.

Our ZUP indicator is:

ZUP_v113wsv63_HT.ex4

The download link is:

http://harmonicstrader.com/download.php#.VHDbq4vF_T8

The software will automatically install the program to your MT4 platform.

2 TRADING EXAMPLES

The following examples should provide a basis for a high probability trading system.

Novice Traders:

I'm trying to keep this as simple as possible. Forex trading is not easy. This particular trading system is the most dependable and easiest to implement. Be very careful and READ MY OTHER BOOKS to learn about MONEY MANAGEMENT and other important trading factors.

TIP:
 If you are pressed for time, stick to the higher time frames and avoid the 5 minute signals. A 60 minute signal may be valid for hours and a 4 hour signal for a day or so. You need to be on the ball to trade a 5 minute signal. TRADE WITH THE LARGER TREND TO CAPTURE LARGER WINS.

I provide video training on YOUTUBE. Go to their site and enter my name to view these short term trades.

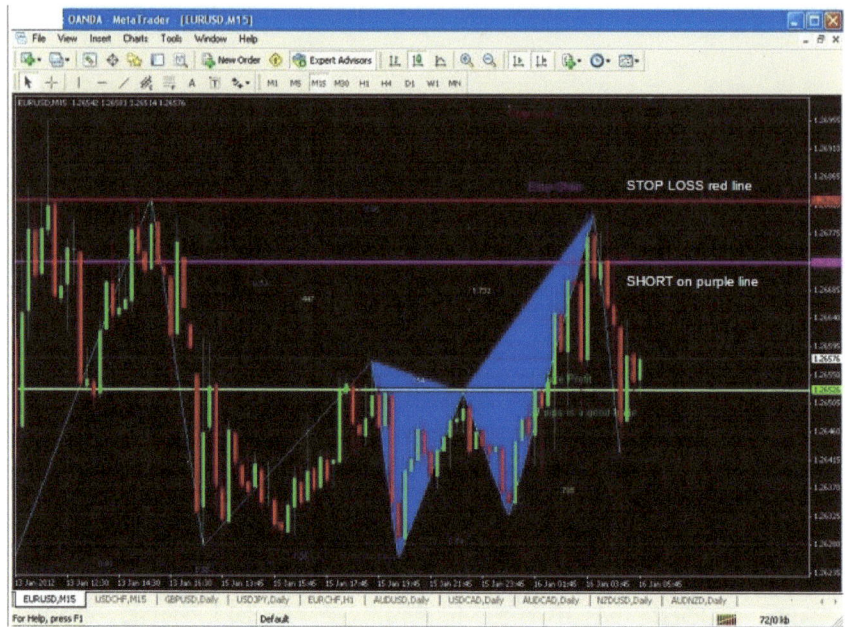

The stop loss is set just above resistance (don't get too close). Tight stops result in frequent losses.

The short entry is set after the move is confirmed. This trade can be set using pending orders with the EASY ORDER TOOL provided later in this book. No need to watch it happen since this will just make you crazy. Take my word for it.

I set the take profit at 20 pips because that is enough for a 15 minute time frame trade. No sense getting greedy.

The entire trade is on AUTO...set it and forget it.

When you return, you will either be up 20 pips or down 10 pips. Win or lose.

These signals provide more wins than losses and the reward/risk ratio is 2/1.

This is is the same trade 45 minutes later. We captured 20 pips profit.

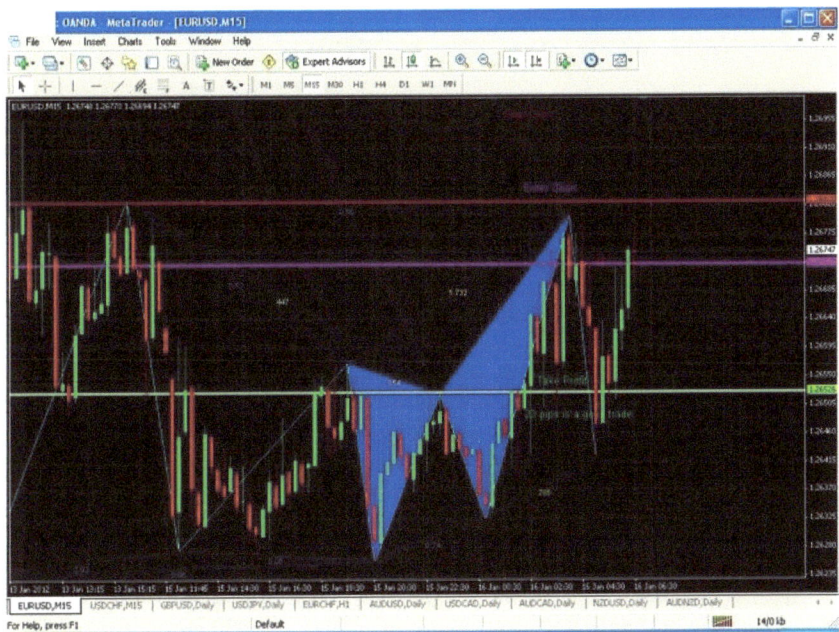

Trade like a sparrow. Take your seed and fly away or the market will eat you alive.

Purple line is ENTRY
Red line is STOP LOSS
Green line is TAKE PROFIT

These levels are fully adjustable using the EASY ORDER TOOL before the trade is entered. Just double click the lines and move them where you want them.

If you insist on watching the trade progress this tool is not necessary.

Here is a 5 minute (time frame) trade in progress. Notice I stand to win far more than I can lose.

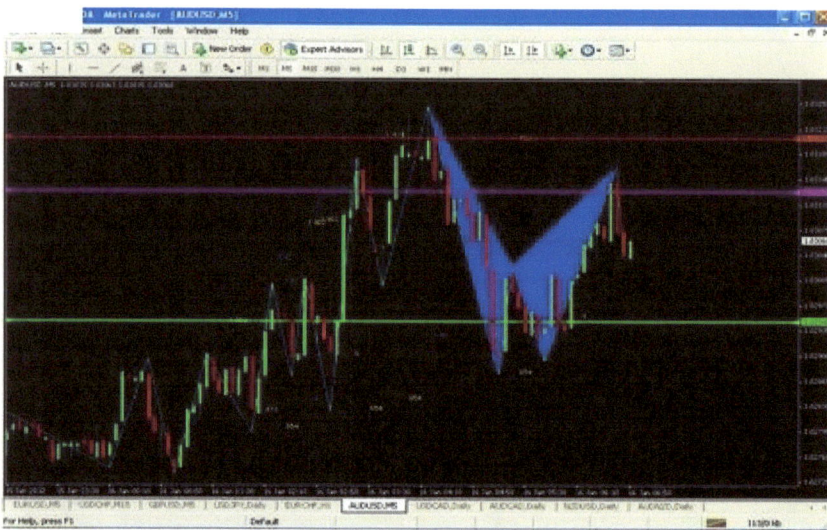

I am trading against the trend on this trade. This often results in a move equal to a fibonacci retracement. I'm not sure this trade will work as planned so I moved my stop loss to a break even point.

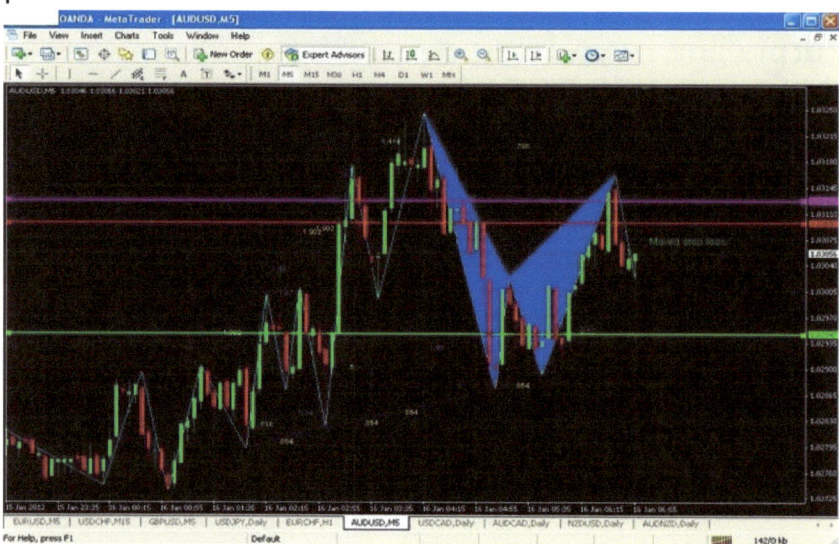

If you control your losses.....the profits will come. 5 minute trades require you to stay close to your trading desk which is the essence of DAY TRADING.
THE STOP LOSS WAS HIT ON THIS TRADE AND I BROKE EVEN.

As I was working on this trade my laptop shut down for no apparent reason. So this is a prime opportunity to say "USE THE EASY ORDER SCRIPT and APPLY STOP LOSS when you enter the trade."

The chart below has been added to make a point. ALWAYS view the BIG PICTURE before trading on lesser timeframes.

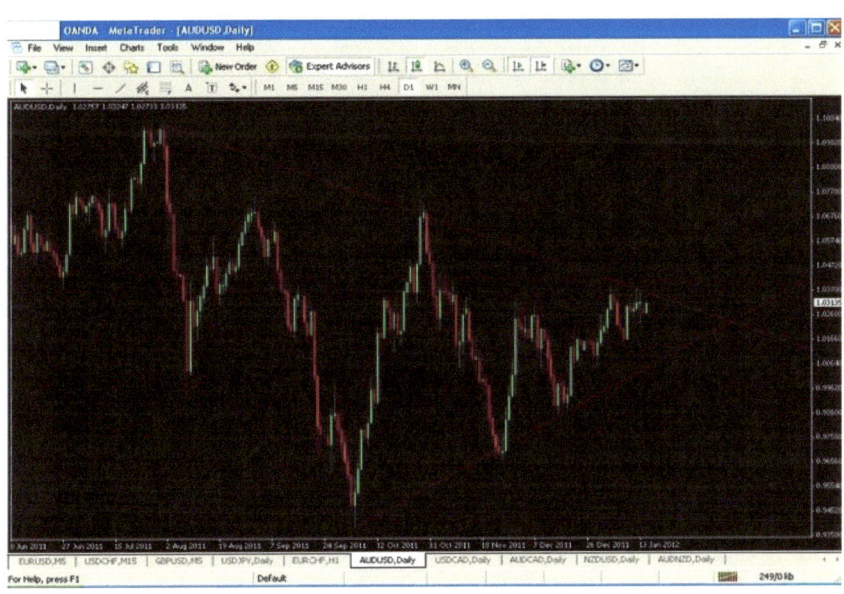

Successful trading requires following rules but after awhile they become second nature and you will do them automatically without thinking. Nothing can replace EXPERIENCE and nobody can make you a good trader. Trade with pennies or dimes when you first start out so you get the feel of losing money and earning money. I NEVER TRADED ON A PRACTICE ACCOUNT. Play money doesn't count and you will learn nothing.

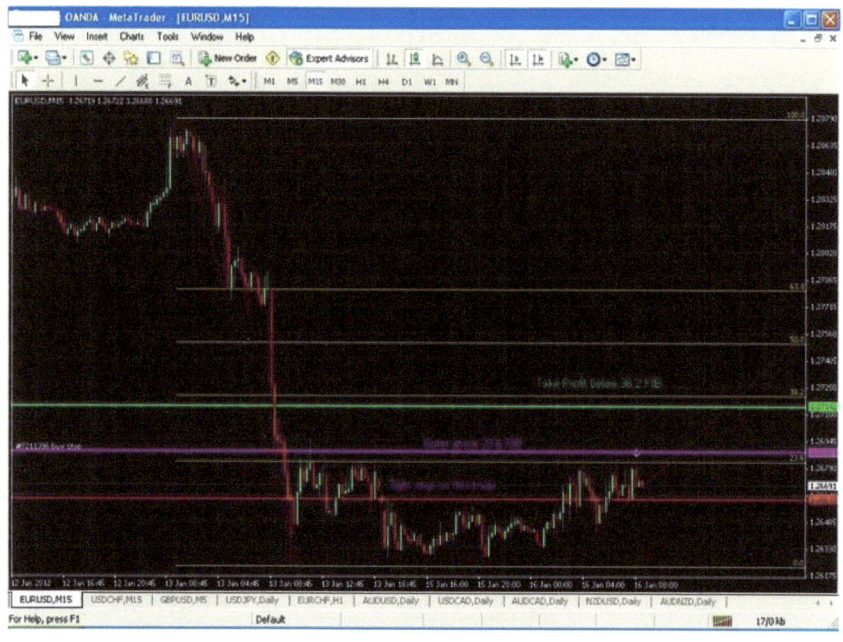

We are trading Fibonacci levels because they are a high probability indicator. The chart above shows the use of the Fibonacci tool.

I give this trade an 80% win probability. If price breaks the 23.6 it should continue on to the 38.2.

If it does not break the 23.6 then I will not be in the trade. Notice my entry and take profit placement.

One hour later. My entry order has not been triggered yet. I,m going to let it stand because these patterns almost always retrace (when you're not looking)

This trade was successful hours later (while I was sleeping).

Never enter a MARKET ORDER, Always enter a PENDING ORDER. Order entry can make you or break you.

All of my trades are conditional. Certain conditions must be met before I enter the trade. This is the only way that you can set up a high probability trade.

The conditions are set up from historical evidence of probable market behavior. Fibonacci levels, support, resistance and trend lines are the triggers for trade entry. They also provide the conditions necessary to set your stop loss.

When setting the stop loss keep in mind that the big traders will usually bump the price action slightly beyond these levels to take out your stop loss. So allow a little room and don't set them too close. You may lose more money but that is the nature of the game.

NEW TRADE AUDUSD 4hour
1) Use EASY ORDER script (double click and move the lines BEFORE you place the trade)
2) ENTER if price drops below the LOW of current bar (something must happen before the trade is entered)
3) TAKE PROFIT placed at SUPPORT
4)Stop Loss is placed above the high of the current bar
5) Trade is now on auto-pilot

The price action on this particular chart may continue UP with the signal remaining valid. If we enter a MARKET ORDER we may have to suffer the drawdown. Use pending orders.

   The 200 day moving average is another indicator used by the institutional traders. When trading the larger timeframes take a quick look at the 200 day moving average.

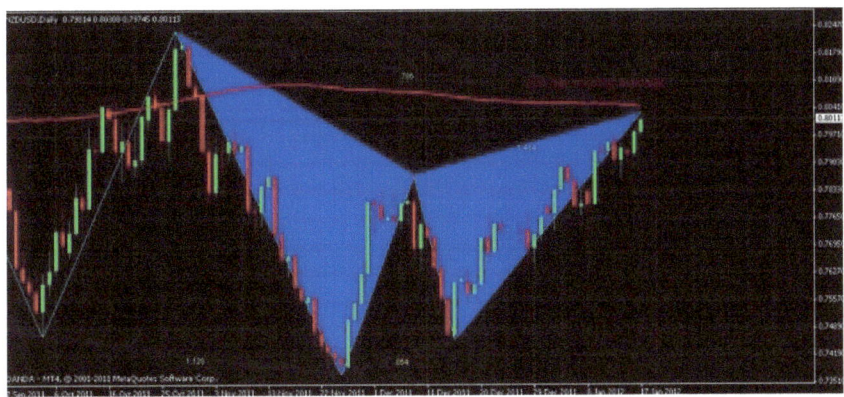

As you can see, our ZUP indicator is calling for a short trade just as the price bounces off the 200 day moving average. This is a very high probability trade.

Waiting for a good trade requires PATIENCE. Slow down and wait for the trade to come to you.

Many novice traders feel the need to be in a trade all of the time. You will be much more profitable if you wait for the perfect set ups. Your money is at risk while in the market. Your money is safe if it is not tied up in a bad trade.

If you allocate your funds to low quality trades you may be unable to jump on a winner when you see one. So be very selective in choosing your trades. Never enter a set up too late and never trade for the sake of trading. There is nothing wrong with sitting on the sidelines.

The following chart is a long term trade on the daily timeframe.

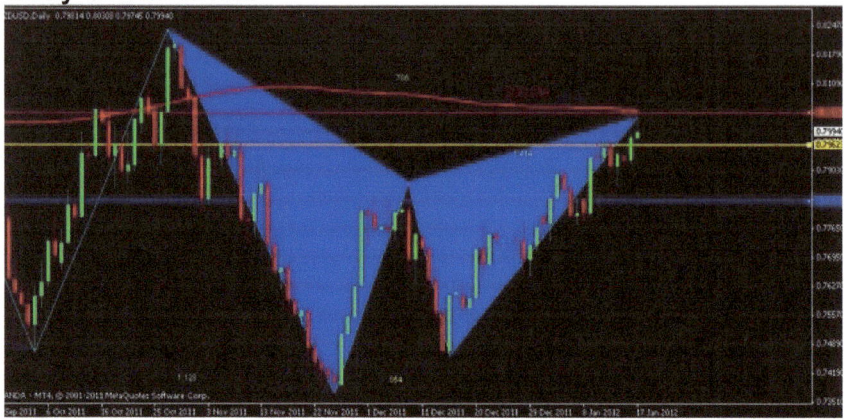

ENTRY: price drops below today's LOW
STOP LOSS: just above today's high
TAKE PROFIT: just above the 38.2 Fibo retracement (fib drawing removed to simplify chart)

24 Hours later: price has moved upward through the 200 MA.....the signal is still valid....I will cancel my pending order and consider the trade again.
THIS IS A PRIME EXAMPLE OF WHY WE DO NOT PLACE MARKET ORDERS !!!
The pending order saved me from entering a losing trade.
The next step is to check the USD against other pairs to determine strength or weakness.
There is no hurry to enter a daily time frame trade (or any trade for that matter).
Hesitation is an asset in forex trading.

Next Day: I set up a new order on this trade

Here is an easy 10 pips on a 15 minute time frame.

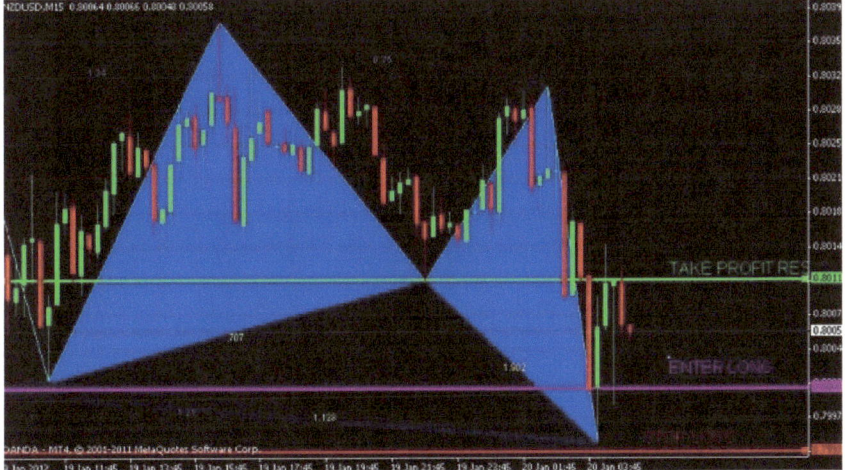

Win 11 pips or lose 8 pips. 15 minute timeframe. Set it and forget it.

10 minutes later: another winner. It bounced dead off the 38.2 FIB

Notice my take profit was just under the fib.

(Both of the above patterns produced 30+ pips).

Here is an easy trade on GBPUSD,

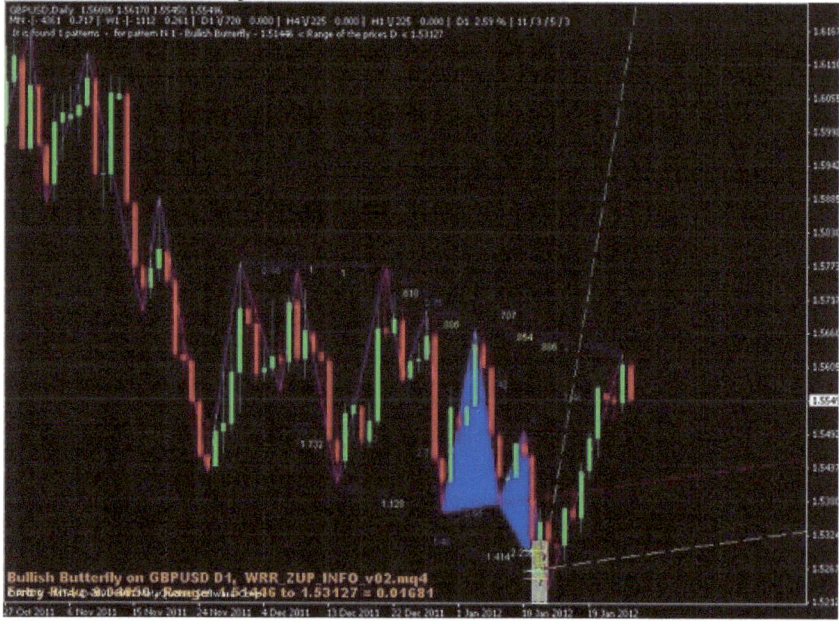

These signals produce 70% winning trades.

This signal is not well defined but I wanted to trade the FIB retracement

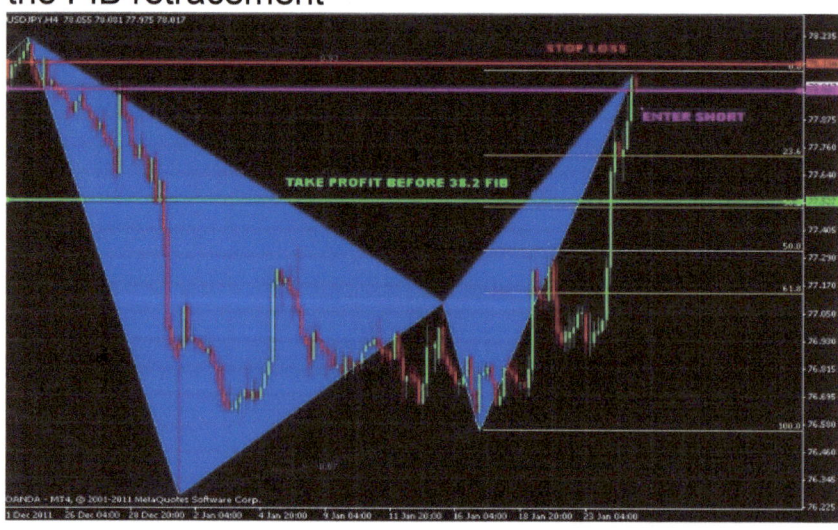

18

After viewing the daily chart, I decided to place a BUY STOP AND A SELL STOP using the EASY ORDER TOOL. Double click the horizontal lines and adjust your trade before you place the order. USDJPY is wild. A lot of central bank activity on this pair (manipulation). Be careful........they want to steal your money.

Learn your orders. You can't trade if you don't know how to order. I explain order types in my other publications.

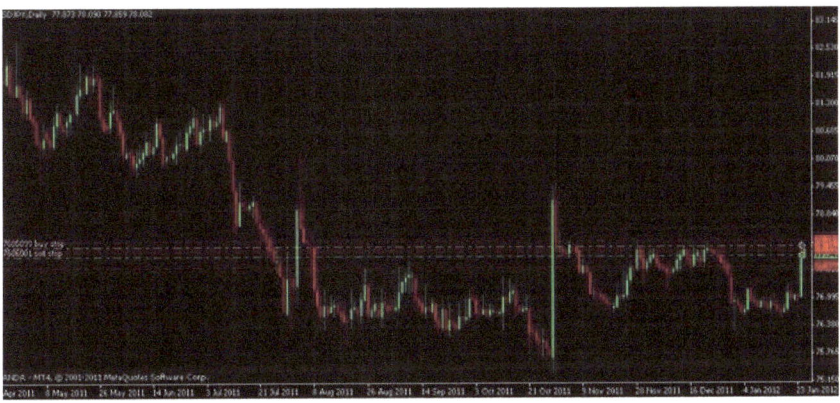

"They" know what you are looking for. They will trap you and trick you if you give them a chance. Fear is a good thing when you enter the market. Be very careful to have stops in place BEFORE you start punching buttons.

Certain pairs are more volatile than others. Get informed at sites such as: Oanda, ForexFactory, and Metaf.net

On this chart THE TREND IS UP and THE SIGNAL IS SHORT. If I were to take this trade, the most I could expect is a FIB retracement of the most recent move. I caught the signal too late and did not take the trade.
NEVER BE IN A HURRY TO ENTER A TRADE. More opportunities will come.

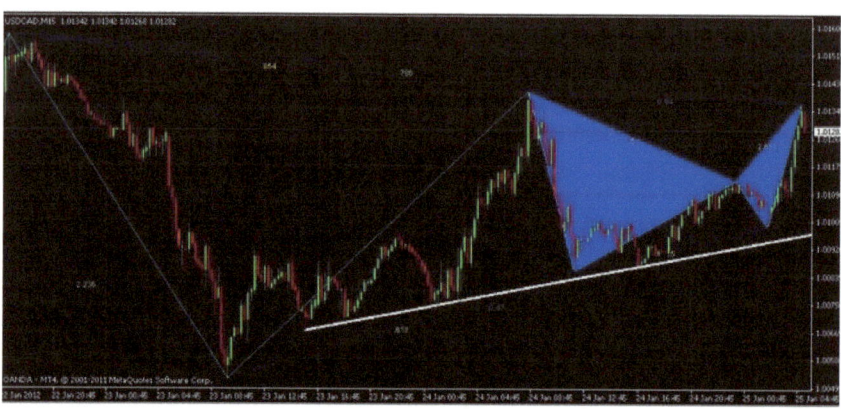

Overtrading is bad. Wait for the BEST trade set-ups. You will have many trades to choose from.....every day. Select only the best.....I can't do it for you because I don't have time. I'm trying to teach you to do it yourself. Then you will be a great trader.

Forex risk aversion tactics:
Forex trading may carry more risk than any other form of market trading. Since the subject of this book is forex spot trading, our risk aversion tactics will be limited to system trading. US brokers no longer support hedging. In my opinion, opening a long and short position on the same pair is not hedging. A true hedge will have the capability to produce a profit.

Profitable hedge trading can be accomplished with options or spreads. I have run across hedge trading strategies on the Forex Factory forums. These strategies use highly correlated or non-correlated forex pairs. I have tested these strategies and they work very well under the right market conditions.

While I'm on the subject, All worthy forex trading strategies work well under the RIGHT MARKET CONDITIONS and none of them work under the wrong market conditions. Our reversal trading system works most of the time, even under the wrong market conditions.

What are the right conditions for harmonic trading?

1) Harmonic trading works very well in range bound markets. This is when the price oscillates up and down within a defined range, commonly referred to as consolidation.

2) Trending markets present two distinct opportunities.

A) A signal in the same direction as the trend will have unlimited profit potential.

B) A signal against the trend presents two distinct opportunities.

a) The maximum profit will be determined by the scope of a Fibonacci retracement or

b) The market is in full reversal which will produce unlimited profit potential

3) The third condition is a failed signal which happens 10 to 20% of the time.

Getting back to risk aversion........it is already built into the trading system. The very nature of trading price reversals gives us a well defined stop loss. The projected take profit should be greater than the possible loss.

The most difficult part of trading any system is FOLLOWING THE RULES. We must eliminate fear, greed, and emotion. That is why I prefer the "set it and forget it" method of trading. Even after 20 years of trading.......emotions still get in the way.

One hour timeframe. GBPUSD
I am trading the fibo retracement. These trades are virtually stress free. Set it and check back tomorrow.

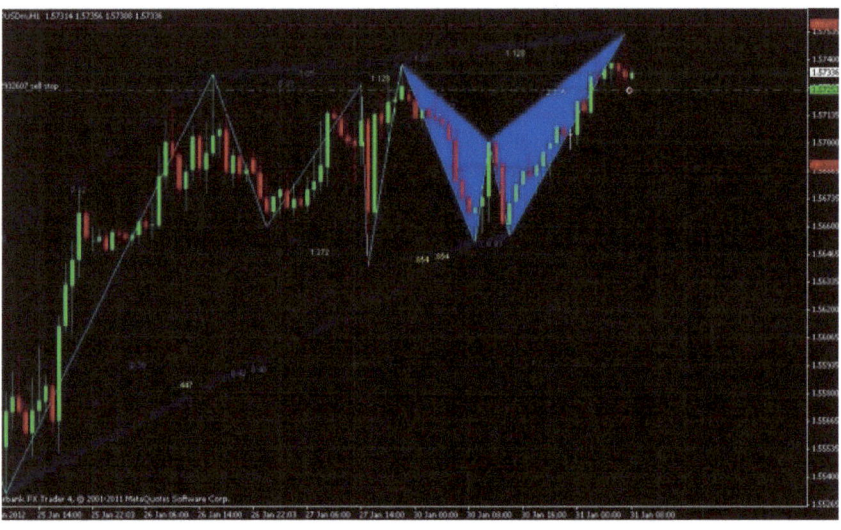

This ZUP indicator is reliable time after time. Over the years I have developed many trading systems. This is the most reliable indicator that I have encountered. I prefer reversal trading over trend trading because of the tight stops.

If you are trading stocks, forex, or futures a signal based trading system might save countless hours of study time. Timing your trade is vital in creating a effective trading system. Online signal providers may eliminate the significant time it takes to follow the markets and time the trade.

Trading signals are useful in trade time but cannot change a great systematic plan. Many amateur traders expect the signal service to complete most of the trading for them. Unfortunately, this isn't the case. It is essential to develop skills related to money management, probabilities, and the risk/reward picture.

With out a money management strategy the investor may ultimately fail. A plan must be developed by the trader to allocate resources based on possible losses.Novice investors are far more worried about how much they could make on a trade. They should also get worried with simply how much they could lose on a trade. Allocating resources equally among deals is an excellent start. For example, the trader may decide that the maximum loss per trade may be 3% of the total account value.

Once the trader enters a posture a stop loss order must also be initiated. In case a certain sum of money has been lost the position will be automatically exited by this stop order. In the aforementioned case, once 3% of the account value has been lost the trade is going to be closed. Buyers should recognize the fact a portion of positions will undoubtedly be loosers whichever signal program they are using.

Trading signals are derived from probabilities. Do the math. This may be described as a spectacular effect, If a investor were to build up a system that had a 50% win percentage and paid out $100 for each win and $50 for each loss. Several signal providers offer signals that produce 80% or greater champions. Since they will not control themselves enough to stick to a solid money management strategy novice traders still manage to lose money.

The investor must trigger the money management program, learn how to trade it, and select a signal service. Exit strategies are required two by every trade. The first exit could be the stop loss. This is on the trade the maximum amount we will drop. If a signal includes a gain ratio of 75% then we know it'll fail 25% of times.

The signal company may both give the stop loss leave to you or show you to ascertain your own stop loss point. It is exactly the same with the profit target. The "learn and earn" method is preferred by me. The trader must just take an energetic part and participate in the trade. Nobody is going to cause you to get rich.

The next exit strategy may be the targeted gain. The gain target might not be the most profit that would be made however it is normally a satisfactory profit target. On any trade the trader will rarely get the maximum win. Suitable win/loss ratios should be applied and considered to each trade. If the entrepreneur enters the trade the loss and expected win is going to be known.

I do not wish to over simplify the trading process but I will offer a simple case. Once the investor enters trade XYZ the results has already been known. The trade will seize a $100 win 75% of the time and experience a $50 loss 25% of the time. If you are not trading in this way it might be time to re-think your practices.

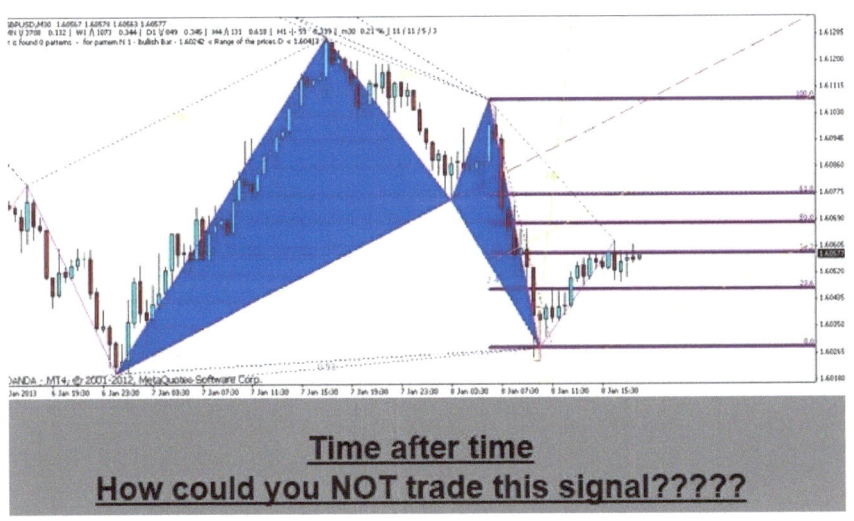

Time after time
How could you NOT trade this signal?????

These signals can also be applied to stocks and futures markets. If you live outside the USA the MT4 platform also accommodates CFDs or Contract for Difference. This trading venue applies CFDs to various stocks and commodities.

Us residents are not permitted to trade this instrument or to trade offshore in general. However, there is no law against using the offshore platform for research. You could do your research on the MT4 and make the trades with a US regulated broker.

This is how to do it. Download the MT4 platform from Insta Trader. Since they are not permitted to accept your trades, you will have to check the box saying that you are not a us citizen or you won't be able to download the platform.

Next right click on the Market Watch menu and select "show all". Now you will have a number of stocks and commodities to apply our ZUP indicator to. You can get your signals from this platform and make your trades with a US regulated broker.

There are a number of offshore brokers that offer CDFs. Any one will do if they offer the MT4 trading platform. Just remember, they are not permitted to business with you and you are not permitted to do business with them. So you can only open a practice account.

Wallmart daily chart.

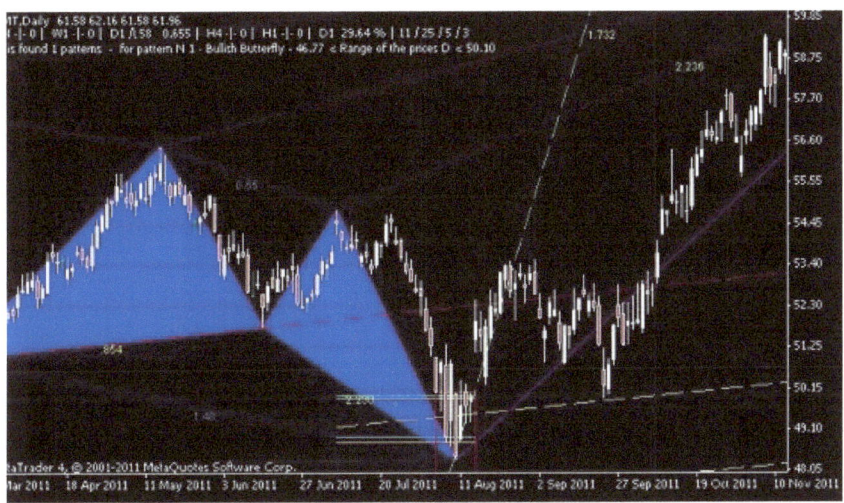

Gold daily chart.

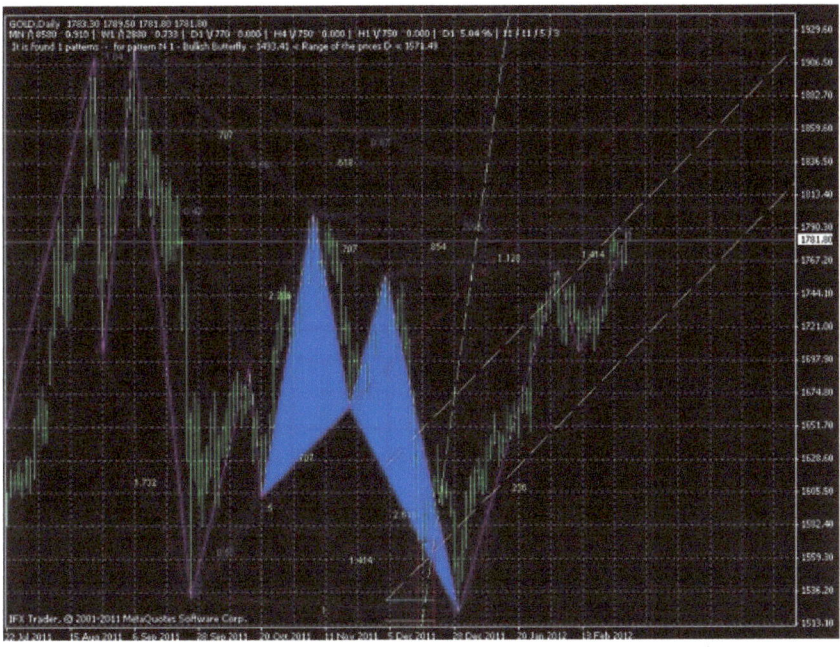

QQQ daily

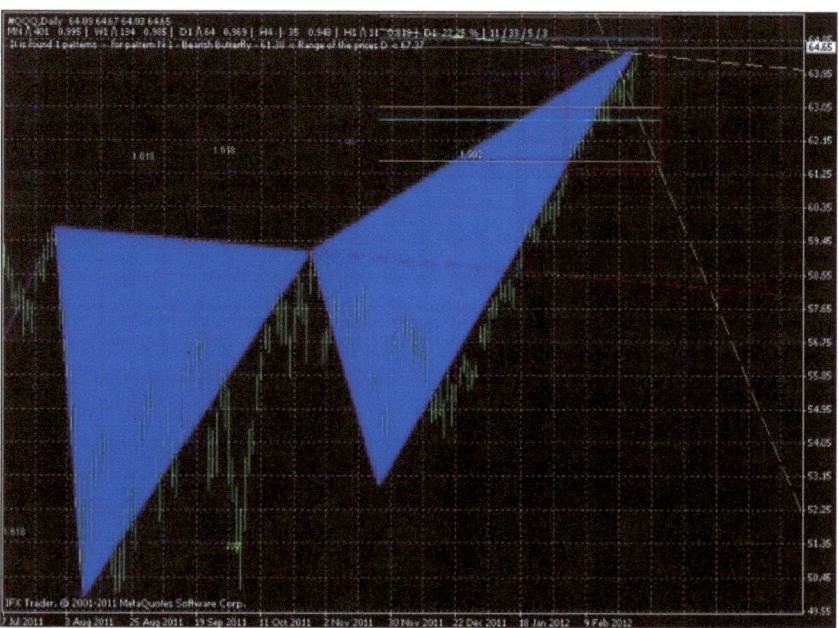

These are TYPICAL signals generated by the ZUP algorithm. The signals are generated many times per week

The one hour signals generate trades lasting one to three days.

The four hour signal generates trades lasting up to a week.

Daily trades may last for weeks or months.

These are all short term, swing trading opportunities based on market reversal.

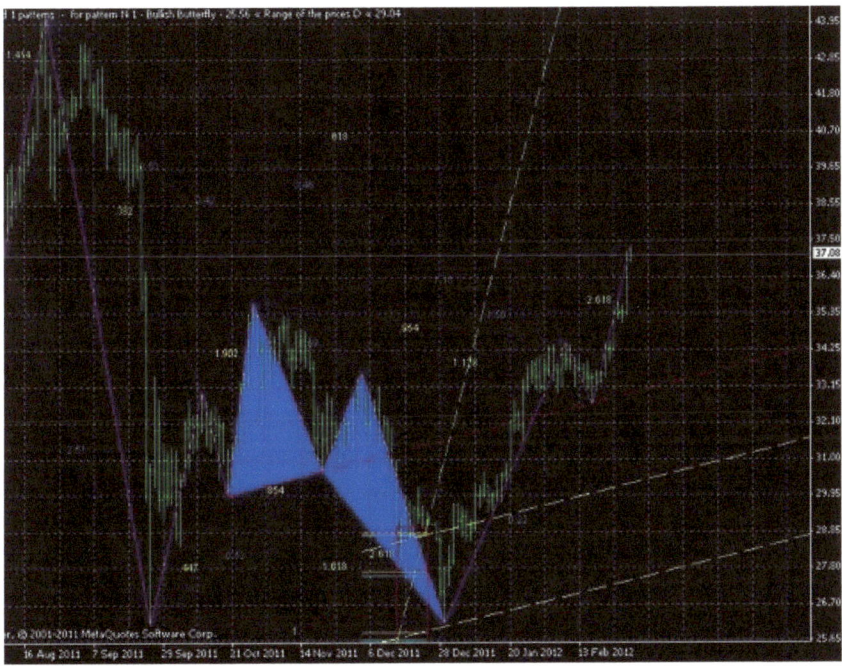

Fibonacci trading has been around a long time.
It is the trading of Fibonacci ratios.

Fibonacci ratios exist in all markets and in all time frames.

The formula used to generate these signals requires a great deal of computer memory. Be careful not to have too many stock or forex pairs running at the same time. It could shut down the program or worse yet, crash your computer.

SPY 4 hour time frame

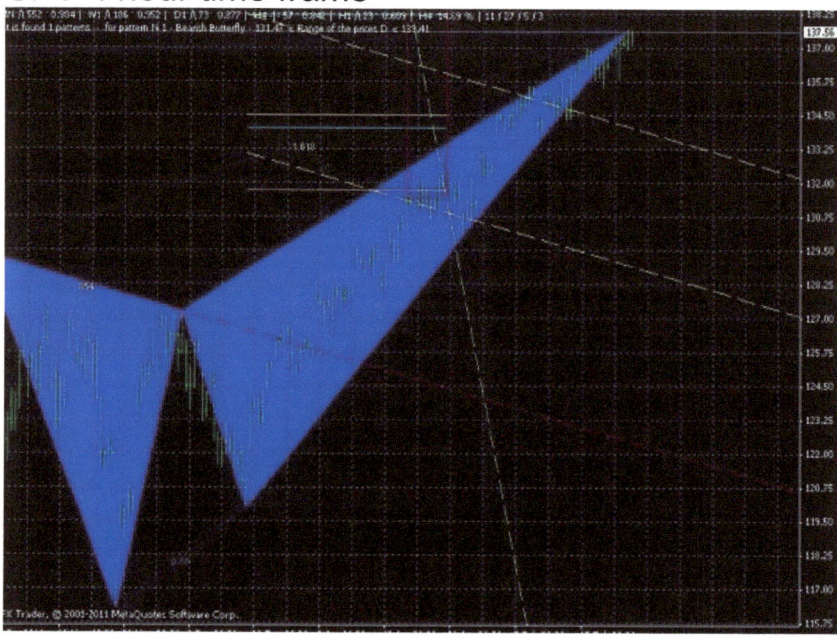

Gold one hour time frame

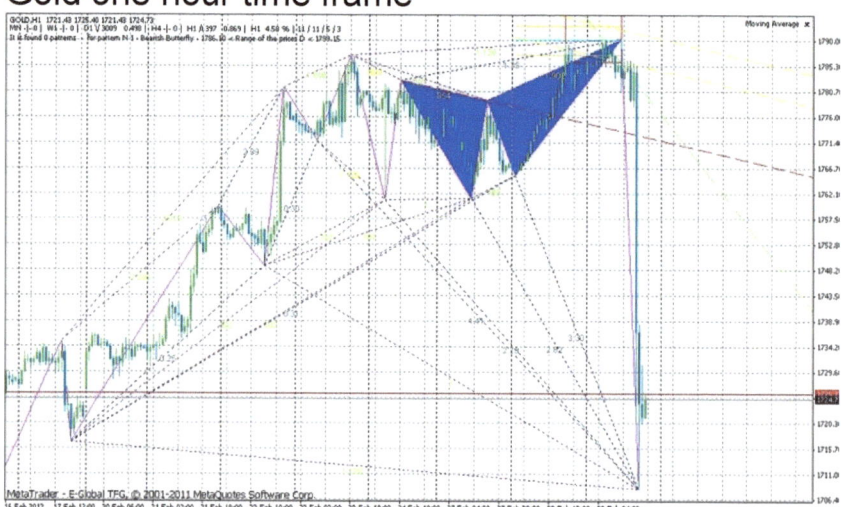

Always check for areas of SUPPORT and RESISTANCE. Trading with the trend will provide greater profits but counter trend signals work equally well. I usually set a Fibonacci retracement exit when trading counter-trend.

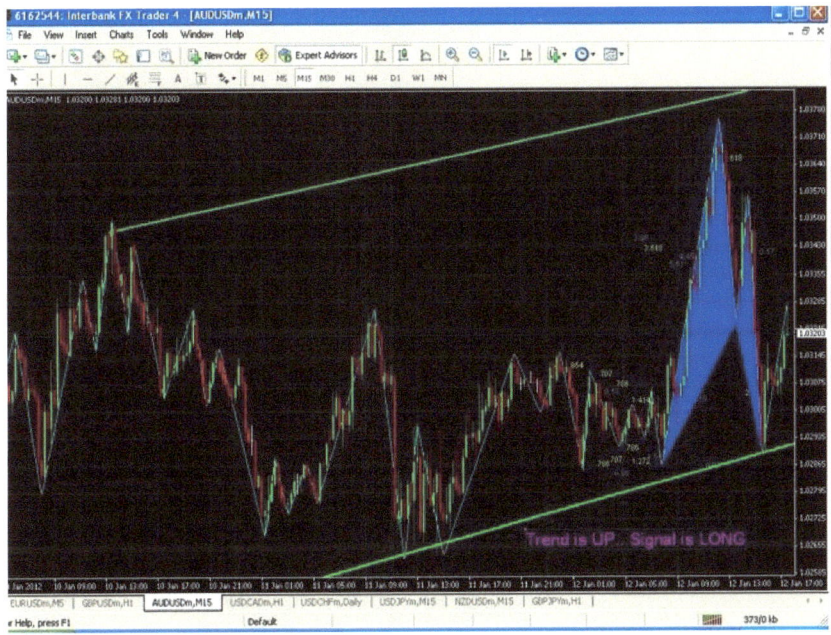

3 FREE TOOLS FOR MT 4

Here are some links to the best free charting and trading tools for the MT 4 platform.

This tool can auto draw support and resistance lines in multiple time frames.

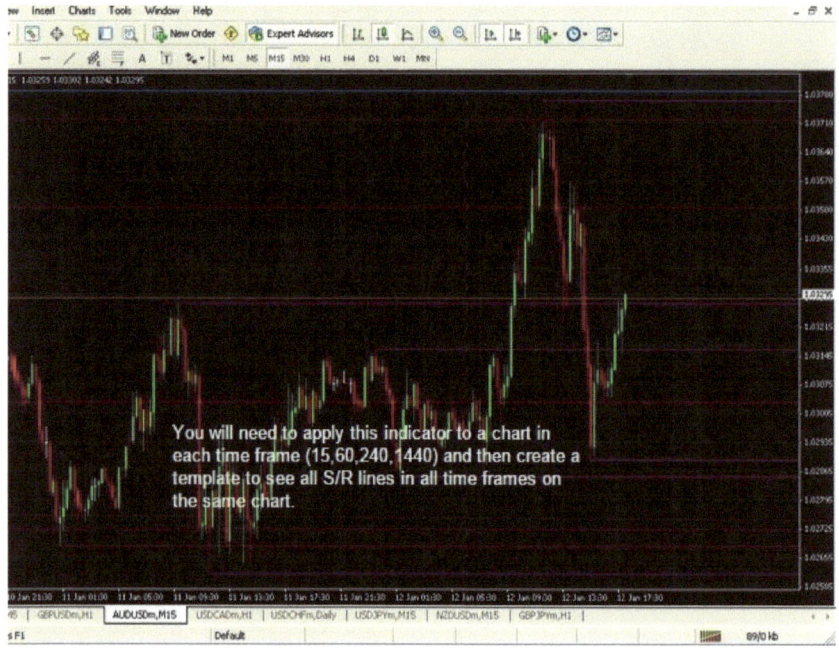

Find it at ForexFactory
http://www.forexfactory.com/showthread.php?t=35224

This tool draws trend lines for you, some you may have overlooked. It can also function in multiple timeframes.

Find it on the MT 4 website.

https://www.mql5.com/en/code/8125

This tool will auto draw Fibonacci levels for you.

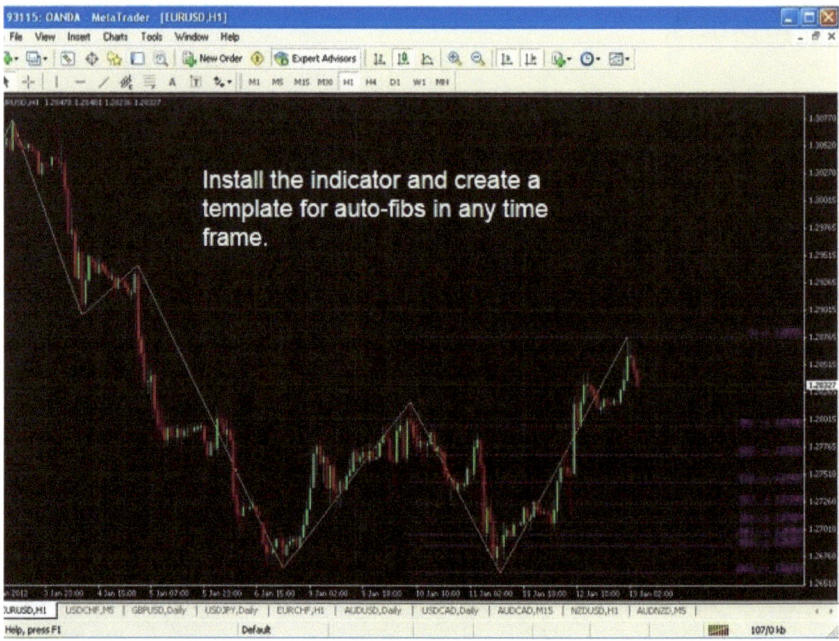

Find it on the MT 5 website:

https://www.mql5.com/ru/code/8257

Here is the EASY ORDER SCRIPT. You can set up the complete trade before entering including the entry, the stop loss, and the take profit level.

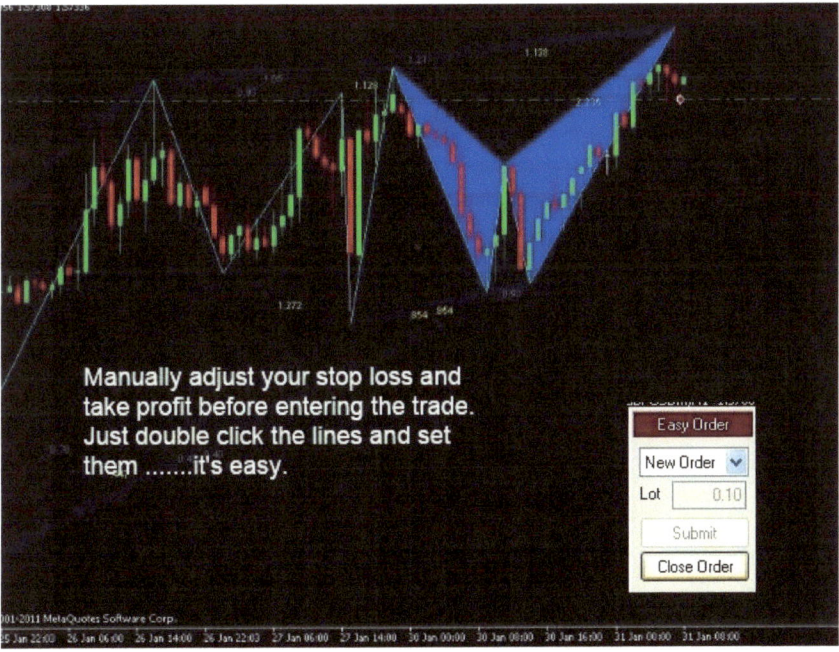

You can find the link at ForexFactory:

http://www.forexfactory.com/showthread.php?t=281772

Here is a relative strength indicator. It will show you which currencies are getting stronger or weaker.

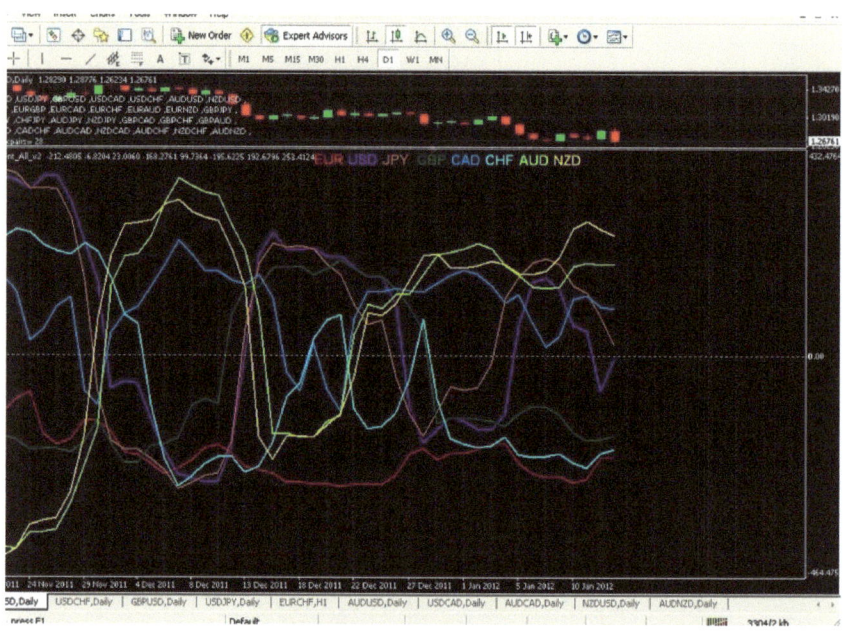

Find the link on ForexFactory:

http://www.forexfactory.com/showthread.php?t=132537

The iVAR indicator is a pattern filter to help determine signal strength.

Closer to 0 implies a price reversal (what we are trading)

Closer to 1 implies a price continuation (weak signal)

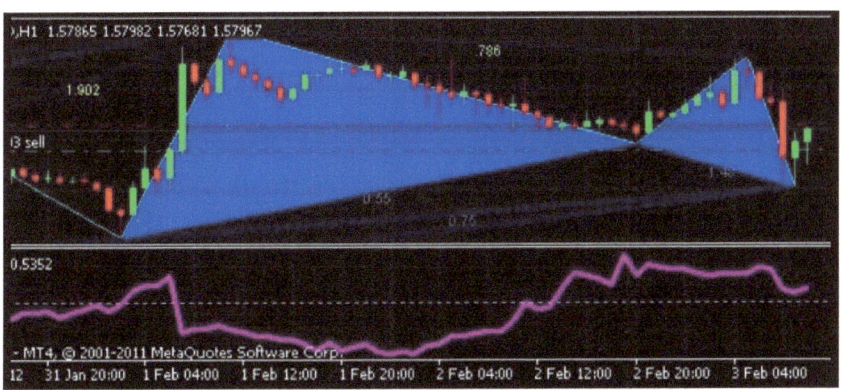

Get the link at ForexFactory

http://www.forexfactory.com/showthread.php?t=166155&highlight=gartley+pattern&page=17

The ZUP INFO indicator can help determine the extent of RISK before entering a trade or , more accurately, the extent of DRAWDOWN before pattern failure.

Find the link on ForexFactory:

http://www.forexfactory.com/showthread.php?t=92292

4 SEASONAL CONSIDERATIONS

Seasonal analysis will enhance the trading system.

The following futures charts might give the trader a "heads up" on future trends. Trading with a bias is acceptable on longer term trades.

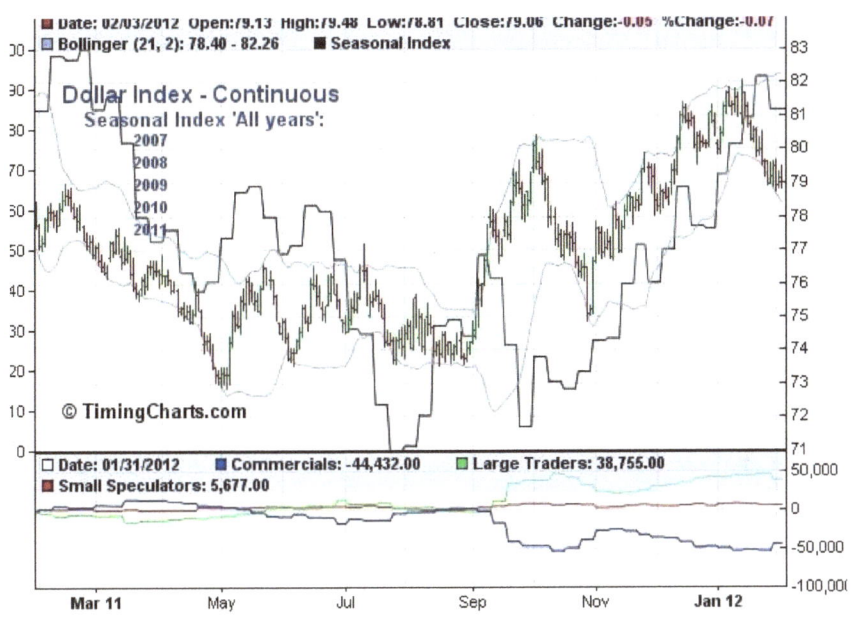

When trading the forex market the dollar rules.

I always check on dollar strength before entering a trade.

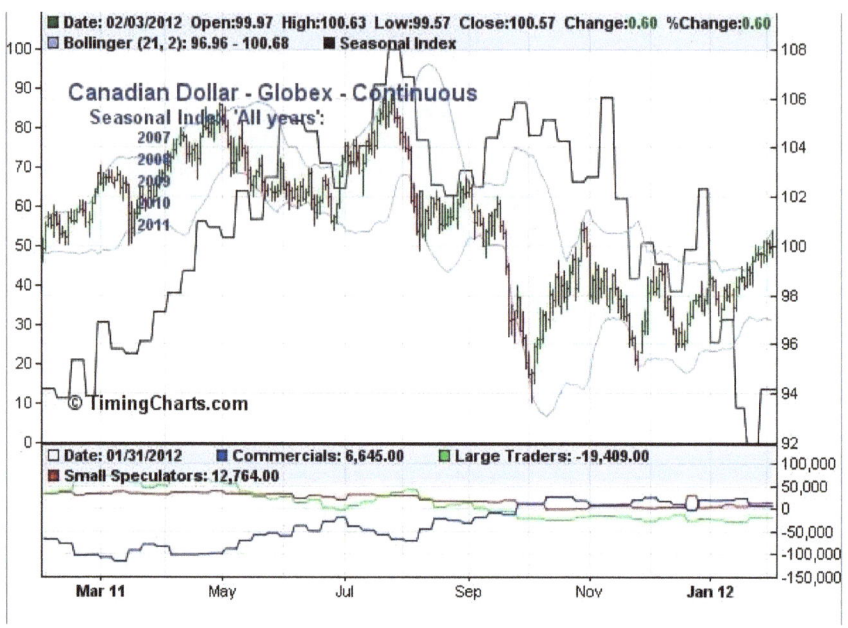

5 MARKET TIMING TRICK

Draw your own conclusion on the charts below. The reversal timing is based on the random selection of a high and low pivot point.

Simply draw a square......when the square ends.....the price will reverse direction. It works too many times to be a coincidence. Works in all markets. I don't know why.

These are just random charts I pulled up. Warning: this is not a trading system.......just fooling around with interesting possibilities.

The "squares" were square when I drew them but did not show up well when transferring the image to the book

Works best on lower time frames due to chart scaling. The squares may not look "Square" on these reproduced photos. One to one chart scaling is available on the MT4 platform, but the higher time frames will not fit on your screen.

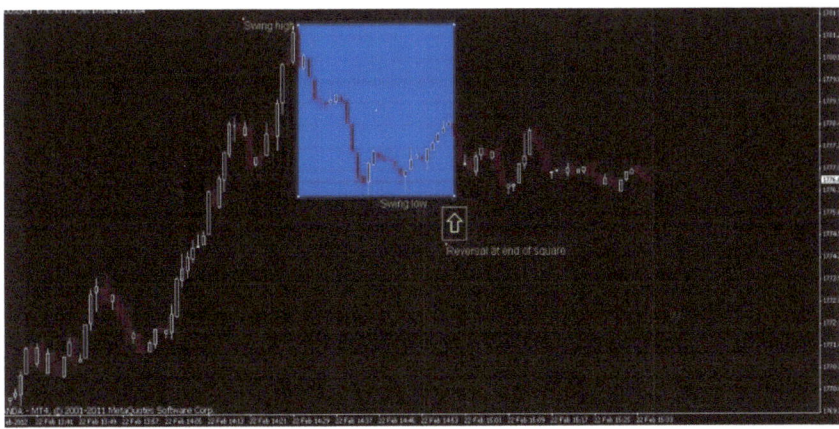

The reversal is not necessarily a big move. The next 3 images were taken from the same chart.
I use a ruler to make sure the rectangle is "square".

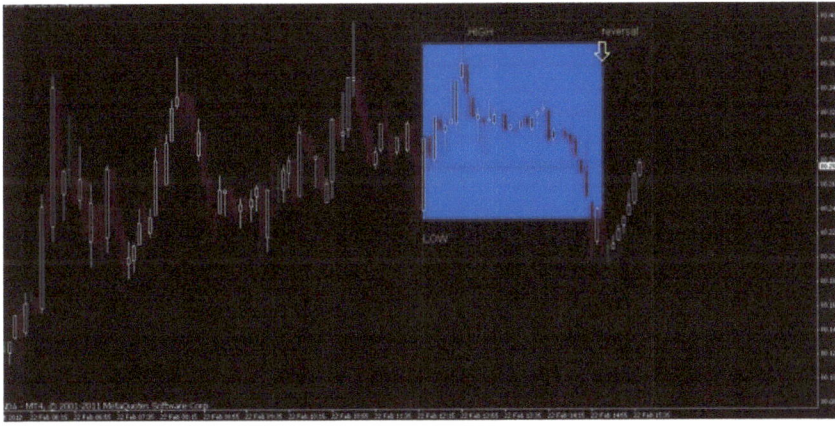

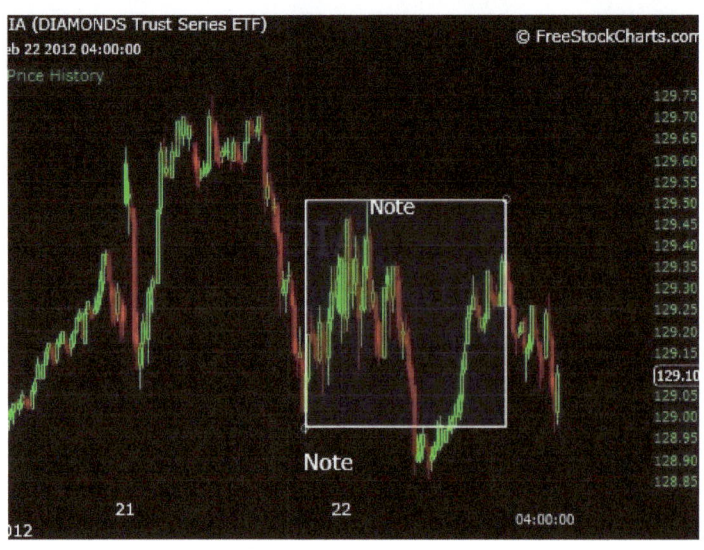

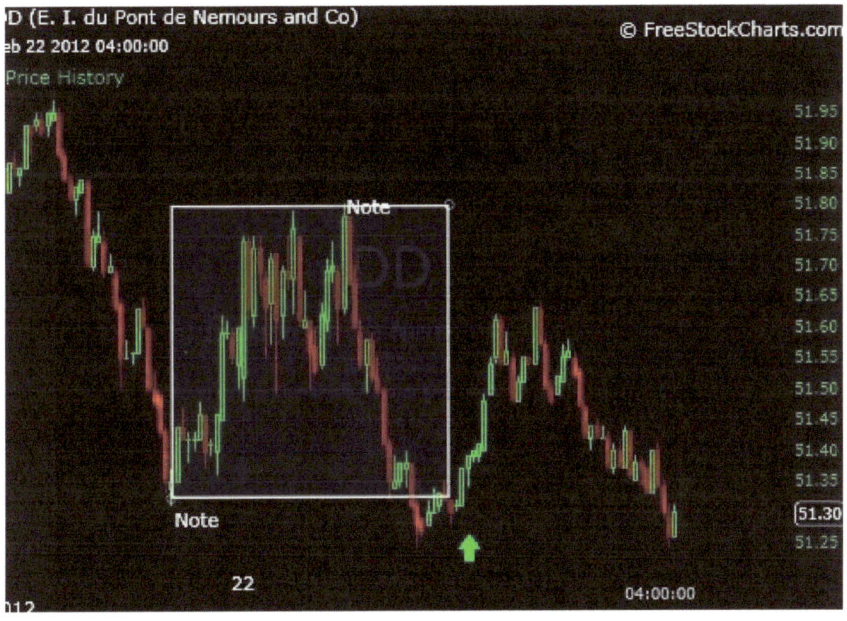

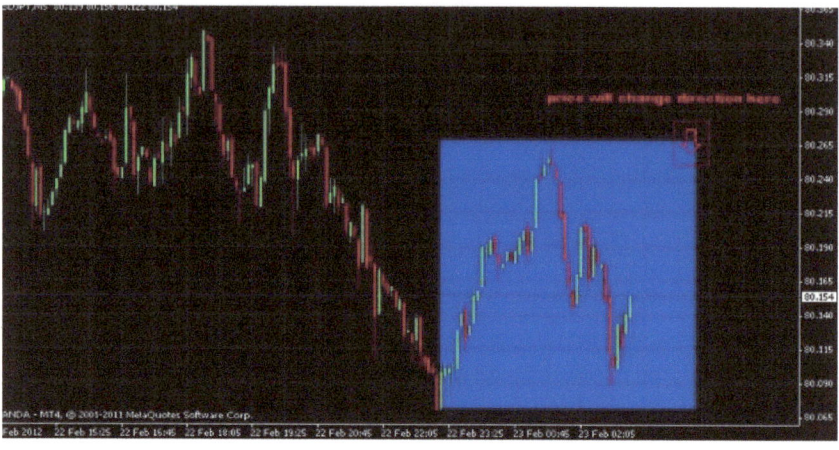

Here is the same chart later on. It wasn't much of a price move....but it did change direction.

Dana DeCecco

Dana DeCecco

www.ingramcontent.com/pod-product-compliance
Lightning Source LLC
Chambersburg PA
CBHW040849180526
45159CB00001B/368